MW01172100

JFK

The
Magnificent
Journey

Alen J. Salerian, Painter

Exhibitions:

Watergate Gallery, Washington, DC
Cartoons: *"Honest Moments with Dr. Shrink"* (2006)

JFK Gallery – Salerian Center, Washington, DC
"JFK's Magnificent Journey" (2007)

National Press Club, Washington, DC
"The Death of JFK", Prof. Fetzer with paintings (2007)

NBC Asman Gallery, Washington, DC
"JFK's Magnificent Journey" (November 2009)

Women's National Democratic Club, Washington, DC
"JFK's Magnificent Journey" (December 2009)

Dealey Plaza, Dallas Texas
"JFK's Magnificent Journey" (May 2011)

Bobby Muller, co-recipient of the Nobel Peace Prize (1997), observed, *"These paintings represent the passion of the artist his search of history for honesty and integrity and accountability. He is the Diogenes of our time."*

Norman Mailer, celebrated author, said of his work, *"Here is one psychiatrist with roaring rage at psychiatric cant and it comes out in a caterwauling fury, which clears the air and enlivens one with its daring."*

About the artist

Washington psychiatrist, Alen J. Salerian, son of Kristin Saleri, an internationally recognized painter, first entered "the fine-arts stage" in 2007 in Washington, DC, with striking blasts of color and energy on canvas depicting JFK's extraordinary life.

JFK
The
Magnificent
Journey

by Alen J. Salerian, MD

SALERIAN WORKS

JFK: The Magnificent Journey
ISBN 978-1516909162 Hard Copy Soft Cover Book

Cover design and layout by Ole Dammegård

Disclaimer and Reader Agreement

Reader Agreement for Accessing This Book

For Kaleigh,

A High School Student

I Dream Thinking

IN MEMORY OF JFK

Dreaming often
I dream thinking
Remembering JFK
Of simple things
Simple wishes of life

Should I be dreaming
Pink red orange
Vibrant colors
Traveling to stars
Impossible things
Inconceivable perhaps
Unnatural by nature
Never occurred on earth
Never before never once

Should I be dream free
Should I let my dreams flee
My government
Civil servants
My president being honest
Zero tolerance for lies
About big things
War and peace
Simple things
I shall dream
Zero big lies
I shall dream

Contents

Foreword

Alen J. Salerian, M.D., has been a champion of the rights of human beings to be alleviated from the suffering they endure as a consequence of mental and physical pain.

This book follows in that tradition by attempting to alleviate the pain and suffering Americans have endured as a consequence of the death of our 35th President.

JFK was no ordinary man, but one of extraordinary intelligence and perception, who had the ability to transcend his own membership in the elite of the United States and extend himself on behalf of every citizen.

Those who advance the interests of their own economic (political, racial or religious) group are dime a dozen. Those who can rise above their own circumstances to act on behalf of every other human being are extremely rare.

JFK was a man of that kind. And I applaud Alen's efforts to explain—in plain and simple language—why JFK's life and death should matter to each of us, even though he was taken out more than 50 years ago.

Because Alen is a psychiatrist who has served as the Chief Consultant for the FBI during his career, he provides a perspective that no other author on this case—and there have been many!—has been able to supply.

This is a modest and unpretentious book, but it packs a punch. By the time you have made your way to the end, you understand what happened to JFK—and why he was taken out. All in all, a remarkable achievement.

What he has written should interest the young and the old, the rich and the poor, working men and capitalists alike. Something extraordinary was lost in Dallas that day, which we must strive to recapture and never forget.

James H. Fetzer, Ph.D.
McKnight Professor Emeritus
University of Minnesota Duluth

Preface

There are two worlds and two Americas: before and after JFK. We observe the changes in our lives, on daily news from around the world. There is hardly anything that happens in daily life on the globe that has not been touched by distrust of governmental integrity in the aftermath of his assassination.

I was 16, then living in Istanbul, Turkey, and I cried when JFK died. I did not speak English. But JFK had given me — and the rest of the planet — hope for a better world.

My feeling was profound, but I did not know why JFK had provided such profound inspiration for a better world. That was something I would only learn several decades later.

Sometime in the early 2000s, I studied the JFK White House tapes of the Cuban missile crises. It was for a possible movie project. The focus was on JFK's mental state during the nuclear confrontation. Had there been any ill effects from his well-publicized medical challenges, as diverse as Addison's disease, chronic back problems and the many medications he had been taking?

JFK was sharp in his mastery of the complexities faced by both sides. His questions were incisive and thoughtful. He questioned with clarity. He understood the complexities of his adversaries as well as the differences within his staff. It was an amazing performance of greatness to firmly promote reason before war and circumvent nuclear catastrophe.

The highlight of the tape was his dialogue with Gen. Curtis LeMay, a staunch advocate of a nuclear attack on the Soviet Union. JFK asked, How would the Soviets retaliate to a potential US nuclear attack? "Nothing to worry about", LeMay replied, "because there will be no Soviet Union to retaliate".

He was terribly wrong. Gen. LeMay did not know of the enormous nuclear capability of Soviet submarines, which were stationed off the coast of North Carolina—ready to launch an attack.

The history books would note that Fidel Castro had already informed Nikita Khrushchev, the Soviet leader, of his own nation's willingness to be nuked to punish the American aggression. Indeed, he was urging the Soviets to strike first.

Khrushchev therefore deserves much credit for the eventual peaceful outcome. The civilian losses for the US and the Soviet Union would have been truly catastrophic, projected to be 10 times worse than the human losses suffered in Nagasaki and Hiroshima combined.

In short, JFK was brilliant in dealing with the gravest crisis to confront the modern world. He must be viewed as a real-life Superman for his leadership to prevent a nuclear war. Sadly, November 22, 1963, canceled his orders to disengage our military involvement in Vietnam. which Lyndon Johnson immediately reversed.

The production of this book has been both painful and rewarding. Many people were crucial to its completion. Bethany Hass, Gregory Salerian and Ara Salerian have helped greatly. James Fetzer and his wisdom and knowledge have been of enormous benefit. Eric Lindstrom was terrific with editorial advice. I almost feel as though they should be co-authors.

Alen J. Salerian, M.D.
Bethesda, Maryland

Dealey Plaza 007

Impossible Dreams

I wish
To be adopted
By sharks and lawyers
Impossible dreams
Tutoring math
Playing the piano
Morality and science
Kindness
Compassion and empathy
Teaching a shark drive a cab
And not eat little fish

I wish to join a tribe
That worships honesty
Bans boxing and lawyers
Partners with
Wild fellows
Honoring handshakes

My wishes
My dreams
Free floating
Wild dreams
Traveling food
For sharks and fish
Unsafe for humans

Introduction

To kill a president is not a difficult job.

To kill a president and get away with it, however, is a very difficult job.

This book is my attempt to provide simple but truthful answers to questions about the death of JFK.

Many people have heard of JFK "conspiracy theories", even if they have only a hazy idea of what they represent. I imagine that most people believe that something horrible with well-organized assassins killed JFK and that THE WARREN REPORT (1964) lacks credibiliy.

We Americans congratulate ourselves on the pursuit of individuality, which places us above all other nations. We see ourselves as champions of freedom, democracy and individual rights. But what may be closer to the truth is that we have not been telling our high school students the facts of the matter.

Truth is complex yet simple. A countless number of extraordinary minds have all greatly contributed to the pieces of the puzzle that I shall attempt to piece together. The unique observations of James Fetzer's MURDER IN DEALEY PLAZA (2000) and of Melanie Mitchell's COMPLEXITY: A GUIDED TOUR (2011) have been of great influence.

The process of understanding gathers momentum gradually with each piece of the puzzle helping to illuminate many other pieces that had not before been fully understood.

In essence, the assassination of John F. Kennedy can be understood through the use of paintings and images.

Truth Is

It's not about football
Doping
Lewinsky affair or Watergate
Epidemics
Measles vaccination and wars
Not about JFK or LBJ
9/11 or 411
Truth is

A Letter to Kaleigh

Doctors For Equal Rights For
Physical And Mental Pain
8409 Carlynn Dr. Bethesda, MD 20817
alensalerian@gmail.com
dralensalerian.blogspot.com

January 26, 2015

Dear Kaleigh,

You are very dear to me. Your youthful bluntness to say what you observe is extraordinarily refreshing. One day, some time after I am gone, you could be our president. I believe you have all the essential gifts to become a president, including the desire to lead.

Please hold on to your values after you enter the White House. Please protect your soul and do not let your triumphs compromise you.

JFK was a great man who defended reason and prevented a nuclear war. He has been my hero ever since.

I want you to watch 6 images and reach your own conclusion about JFK's death. Then write down on a piece of paper, a note to yourself and say, "I will not change when I become the president." Sign it. And remember your pledge.

Here are six images with unusual content:

Each one may be viewed as accidental. Together they make us think of different possibilities:

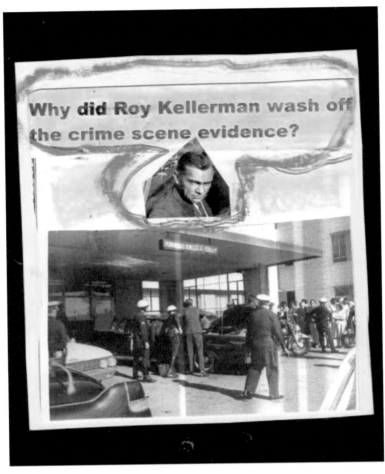

- *Secret Service agents washing off crime scene evidence at Parkland Hospital parking lot before the president died.*

- *Christchurch Star* news reporting the death of President Kennedy before the president died.

• *Capt. Fritz walking away as Jack Ruby killing Lee Harvey Oswald.*

National Security Agency sigint doc from 21/11/63 (21 Nov. '63)

- 0845 (8:45 am) Received APSC message from USO 790 DOD 234792 picked up by Sargent Holtz at 10,000 hours.
- 1310 (1:10pm)- AF SSC SAC message DIG 22342C2
  - GRASS KACS preflight instructions per Mr. Heumer PO4 Hard copy dist 00 A675 6 61 all
- 1335 (1:35pm)- All couriers for weekend cable are briefed
- 1414 (2:14pm)- Sent message to CAG SMMS reporting President Kennedy reported shot
- Received
  - I NDIC msg 76-63 from 011/ CIMC OT6 2219263 advance copies to PCS S40C

• *Top-secret national security memo reporting the death of President Kennedy on November 21, 24 hours before the assassination.*

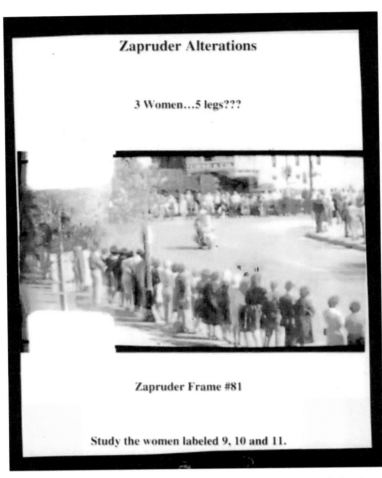

- *Zapruder movie frame number 81 showing two women with five legs.*

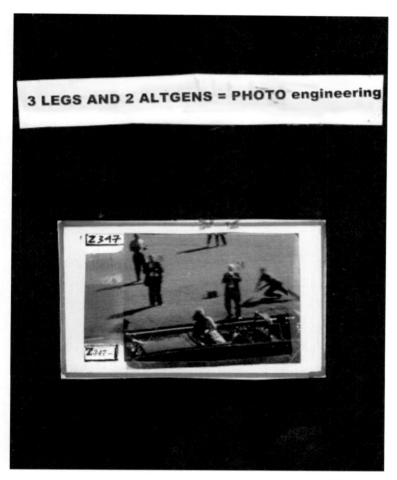

3 LEGS AND 2 ALTGENS = PHOTO engineering

- *Zapruder movie frame 347 showing 3 legs in an open field.*

JFK Spoke To Me

For Jim Fetzer

Yesterday
JFK spoke to me
When blizzard froze
My Washington
Giant oak trees
Whiteness glowing

Yesterday
JFK felt my words
From heaven
My caterwauling fury
At frozen stillness
Excruciatingly slow demise
Of beautiful trees
Choking with no air
Truth
Buried under
Rock solid ice

Yesterday
JFK listened to me carefully
About my worries
Fragile things
Addicts soldiers call miners
Damaged colorful people
Black, Cherokee red
Conspiracy theorists
Prisoners of wars
On distant planets

This morning
JFK spoke to me
"I know who killed me
I can say it, I'm here," he said
Who I shouted
"The King", he said.
Who is the King? I yelled
That's when falling leafs
Began to sing
Fantastic winter sounds
Crescendoing into the sky.

Ch. 1:

Chief Justice Warren vs Mother Oswald

On November 22, 1963, as the presidential limousine traveled on Elm Street in Dealey Plaza, Dallas, Texas, multiple shots were fired, killing President John F. Kennedy and wounding Governor John Connally.

Is it possible to understand what occurred on November 22, 1963 at Dealey Plaza without answering two questions?

1. Whom do you believe: Chief Justice Warren or accused assassin, Lee Oswald's mother, Marguerite?

2. What is complexity?

Let me put the matter in another way. If an engineer is asked to solve why an airplane crashed, you will expect that input from key experts and black box data would be crucial. The input from the Chief Justice and Mother Oswald—along with insights from complexity mirror—what happened to JFK in parallel to an airplane crash.

What did Chief Justice Warren conclude?

On September 24, 1964, after 10 months of secret hearings, Chief Justice Warren presented the Commission's report to President Johnson. The report said that Lee Harvey Oswald, alone, from a 6th floor window of the Texas School Book Depository building, fired three shots with a Mannlicher-Carcanno, killing JFK and wounding Connally

Lee's mother disagreed.

"My son served our country. He should rest at the Arlington national Cemetery", she observed on November 26, 1963. Not even the constant drizzle, nor the dark clouds, nor unfriendly questions about her son would dampen Mrs. Oswald's conviction of her son's innocence.

Naked Village

Why not to build
A different world
One village at a time
A transparent village
Every nail every stone
Glass columns
Civil servants
And the Army
All naked
Naked weapons
No secrets
No secret tools

I have been told
Not to build ships
Glass shIps
Big or small
Armed or disarmed
For voyages in space
Mars Jupiter Saturn
And beyond
Reasons secret
Serious dangers
Epidemics
Unknown dangers

I will build ships
Paper ships
Will paint
Great ships
Might write poems
Titanic Capt. Smith
Heart-wrenching tales
Shall sculpt
Sailing ships
Robust well-built
First-class
I shall invite my friends
For joyrides on my ships
Voyages of joy

Ch. 2:
What is complexity?

The collective performance – invisible or unobservable – of many units to produce a precise outcome. How billions of cells work together for brain function or the extraordinary performance of ant: colonies are good examples of complexity. Complexity in human affairs becomes a conspiracy when it involves collaboration between two or more person to commit a crime, typically designed to remain undiscoverable. This is an essential point.

The perfect conspiracy is difficult to prove or even unprovable because crucial evidence has been eliminated. Since obvious proofs are missing, according to its intelligent design, we must rely on mathematical models and indirect evidence to reconstruct the crime, who was responsible and why it was committed. A revealing illustration is *The Christchurch Star's* report of the President's death

In the morning of November 22, 1963, JFK was waving to exuberant crowds in Dallas, Texas, while New Zealanders were reading the bloody details of his assassination in *The Christchurch Star*. The newspaper had printed the details of the assassination, including the highly sensitive background information on Oswald, the alleged killer, including about his days in the former Soviet Union. Unaware of the published news, JFK frequently stood up and waved during his last journey .

Why? Why? Why? How? How? How?

In 1963, it took at least six hours for any news to be printed and distributed. With the time difference of 12 hours between Dallas and New Zealand it was impossible for the newspaper to publish the assassination and the assassin's background information unless the article had been pre-edited.

The story also contained a minor but a "signature trait error" of complex complicity. It made a reference to the yellow roses that Mrs. Kennedy had received. But in Dallas, her roses were red. They were expected to be yellow but had been changed to red in the last minute. Some observers hypothesize that the change was aimed at saving Mrs. Kennedy from getting shot. Red signified a party who should not be harmed

My Bus Would Come Soon

I have been awaiting
That bus to come
A bus from nowhere
Hoping
A passenger
Will bring pigeons
Many pigeons
Gray black or white
Carrying good news

I have been having
Dreams of freedom
Dreams in which
I will be free
No invisible fences
Gray black or white
Around my neck
No sudden jolts
By restless men
Unnerved by freedom

A bus arrived
This morning
No man no pigeons
A woman
Glowing joy
With triplets dressed
Gray black and white
Smiled at me
As If to say
My bus
Would come soon

A bus arrived this morning
A men with pigeons
High drama excitement
Jumping in the air
Shouting freedom
Dancing crazy
Waking up
A wonderful dream

Ch. 3:
Who was Lee Oswald?

Oswald's life and childhood have been extensively studied with diverse speculations about what might have been mental problems that could explain his role in the assassination. Declaring Oswald guilty without proof would be unwise. Yet, a few basics about Oswald's background are helpful in placing him within the big picture of JFK's death.

Lee Harvey Oswald was born at the old French hospital in New Orleans on October 18, 1939. He was named after his deceased father, Robert Edward Lee Oswald, a life-insurance agent, who ihad been named after the Confederate States General, Robert E. Lee.

Lee had two brothers, John Edward Pic, a half-brother born in 1931; and Robert Oswald, born on April 7, 1934.

The sudden death of Robert E. Lee Oswald from a heart attack induced profound financial and social trauma for Marguerite and the family.

Education and Upbringing

Soon after Lee's birth, Robert and John were sent to a Catholic boarding school, The Infant Jesus College in Algiers, Louisiana. Lillian Murret, Marguerite's sister, babysat with Lee so that Marguerite could work. The babysitting arrangement with Lillian would last until Lee turned three and was placed in The Evangelical Lutheran Bethlehem Orphan Asylum on weekdays.

Lee was five when mother remarried an industrial engineer, Edwin A. Ekdahl, with the family moving to Ft. Worth, Texas. Marital difficulties, however, would force Marguerite and Lee to move to Covington, Louisiana, in 1946. By 1948, divorce came while John was 15, Robert 12 and Lee 9.

By then Lee had already attended three different elementary schools and been diagnosed with dyslexia. He did fine in school academically with an IQ of 103. Despite the social turmoil Lee was observed to be liked by his peers. Phil Vinson, a second grade-class mate, for example, said, "All the boys looked up to Lee."

Life in New York City

First John—and later Robert—would join the military before the family moved to Manhattan, New York, in 1952. John was stationed on Ellis Island. There were conflicts between John's wife, Margie, and Lee and Marguerite. It's impossible to know the details, but we know of another move by Marguerite and Lee to the Bronx in 1953.

This time period would also coincide with Lee's problems in school and, in particular, with his truancy. It's also interesting to note that his IQ was now recorded as 117, which in a higher range, where most of his behavior problems appear to have reflected the conduct of a bright, curious teenager, living in a big city with extremely limited parental supervision.

The medical records—from his stay in a psychiatric facility for adolescents ordered by the New York City Children's Court—suggest neither a wild or crazy kid nor a troubled adolescent with destructive traits. Just the opposite: instead, a curious boy who was finding his way to The Bronx Zoo but was intercepted and shipped to an asylum for kids.

Lee idolized his brothers, who were in the military. He knew what he wanted. He wanted to be like them. He joined the Marines at the age of 17. He had enough self-discipline and perseverance to complete Marine training and even managed to gain fluency in Russian through the military system.

Psychiatric observations

In general—for good scientific and ethical reasons—psychiatry frowns upon psychiatric analysis of people without their consent and void of direct examination. Yet in the spirit of fairness to Oswald and his mother, I would observe that there is nothing in Oswald's background that would suggest he suffered from a psychiatric illness.

Marguerite Oswald has also been portrayed as an uncaring, unstable, bad mother who created a monster. These arguments are simply silly. From the beginning to the end, Marguerite Oswald defended her son and argued for his innocence. Not once did she indicate any doubt about the falsity of the allegations against him.

Was she a troubled woman? Who knows. Was she a bad mother? There is no evidence to support that. We know she worked very hard to provide food and shelter shelter for three children after the tragic death of her husband. From all indications, she seems to have been a caring, loving and loyal mother.

A Baby Dolphin In Tears

Off Outer Banks
A baby dolphin in tears
Mad at sharks
Eating baby sister
Demanding action
Concrete measures
Like kidnapping
The mean sharks
Bringing them to justice

Papa dolphin attentive
Not splashing
Relentless is baby dolphin
"Do we have justice Papa
Are our waters wild west
Have we become humans?"

In one swift move
Lifting him in the air
Inhaling and flying
Papa. dolphin is clear
"Size matters son "
"How about democracy
International treaties
Are they all fake Papa?"
"True but size wins
My baby boy
They eat swim and die
We fly breathe and live
My good boy"

Ch. 4:
Victim of a complex crime?

The possibility of Oswald having been the victim of a complex crime is based upon complexity concepts. I suggest the topic of a complex crime acts as a critical link between observable and unobservable influences. Without a firm grasp of factors that are not easily observable, an adequate investigation of Oswald's role in JFK's death would be impossible.

The focus of this discussion is to start with the basics of the physical impossibility—or virtual impossibility—of numerous events associated with Oswald's arrest and death. We will address different extraordinarily unusual events and failures. We will rely on already established evidence.

The Christchurch Star news about Oswald's presumptive guilt and background having been published before JFK died offers clues. Regardless of why and how it occurred, The *Christchurch Star's* report sticks out as a signature trait of a complex crime by concealed influences.

Oswald as suspect

How, after all, could Oswald have become the prime suspect roughly 70 minutes following the gunfire at Dealey Plaza?

The short but inaccurate answer is that this was a human error, because he was wrongly thought to be the only employee missing from the Texas School Book Depository building after the shooting. Later the records would show that there were seven people missing. Another very unlikely error would also occur with the identification of the weapon allegedly used by Oswald—the Mannlicher-Carcano.

Three Dallas Officers

Three senior Dallas police officers, Craig, Boone and Weitzeman, originally signed affidavits declaring the weapon found in the depository to be a German Mauser. So we already have two major and most unlikely human errors by responsible adults with important jobs.

Then, there is the testimony by Howard Brennon, the sole witness to report having seen Oswald standing in the 6th floor window at the time of shooting. This claim is not rational or believable. The window was not broken and it could only open partially.

For a shooter to aim at JFK from the 6th floor window, he would have to have been on his knees and not standing up. Brennan's identification was too specific and detailed to be credible.

Improbabilities

By was of summary, for Oswald to have been guilty, the following series of mishaps had to have occurred:

(1) an incredible claim by the only witness reporting Oswald at the 6th floor window at the time of the shooting has to be accepted as believable and true;

(2) the preposterous contention of a single bullet having injuring both JFK and Gov. Connally, which turns out to be anatomically impossible, has to be accepted;

(3) the signed affidavits by three senior Dallas police officers identifying the weapon found in the depository as a German Mauser must be ignored;

(4) the false claim of Oswald as having been the only missing employee in the aftermath of the shooting must be accepted as true; and,

(5) evidence uncovered by Waggoner Carr, then Attorney General of Texas, that Oswald had been working for the FBI as an informant has to be discarded.

The truth of any of the these five points is already sufficient to establish Oswald's innocence. That five major flaws coincided to establish Oswald's presumptive guilt means something in the context of complex crimes: complicity!

The physical laws and Oswald's innocence
the motorcycle officers Hargis and Martin were splattered with blood and brain tissue consistent with gunfire from the front with a frontal entry and back exit of a bullet. This suggests, Oswald who was allegedly shot the president from behind is innocent.

M. Grignis drawing

The direct and observable facts also help exonerate Oswald. Motorcycle escort policemen Hargis and Martin were on the left and behind the presidential limousine. They were splattered with blood and brain tissue.

This establishes that the shot that caused that effect came from the front–the grassy knoll or the Triple Underpass—and inflicted a frontal entry wound. With Oswald's position behind the president, we have the most compelling proof that Oswald was not responsible for the head-shot and that THE WARREN REPORT's conclusion was flawed.

Mr. Ass Barks
No Fussing Over Lies

What should I do
When I smell deceit
Can you smile
When you smell stench
Can you play the game
The polite game

My good friend Ass
Suggests no fussing over lies
"Cover up matters
Modern world "Mr. Ass barks
"Don't lose sleep
Over spilled lies"
Mr. Ass barks louder
"When a smart man lies
You're done my friend
The more you unseal
The faster you sink
The louder you yell
The harder you fall "
"How about fairness
And my government ?"I mumble
"Fairness you will have
In heaven
Government likes polite games"
Mr. Ass barks loud
Very very loud

Ch. 5:
How about
THE WARREN REPORT?

Virtually all investigative reports are necessarily based upon information derived from available data. If the data is faulty or incomplete, then the conclusion will almost always be inaccurate. It is easy to understand the flawed conclusions of THE WARREN REPORT based upon the observation that the above summarized findings were not shared with the commission.

There are also other highly suspect actions, which, once again, suggest the influence of unobservable factors dictating the final verdict.

But this book is not about THE WARREN REPORT. Here I shall advance two examples to demonstrate that The Warren Report lacks scientific integrity.

 * The first one the role of Alan Dulles, the former CIA Director, who as fired by JFK yet participated as a key member of the committee. Unethical? Inappropriate? Conflict of interest? Simply wrong?

 * The second one is the "magic bullet" hypothesis. The report concluded that a bullet struck the president then traveled several feet in the air to inflict multiple wounds of Gov. Connally. This explanation sounds as silly now as it did half a century ago.

You may form an opinion about THE WARREN REPORT by realizing that Dulles was an influential member of the committee, who promoted the fantasy of a traveling bullet with an impossible trajectory entering a human body then exiting and reentering another body to shatter a rib and break the wrist of Gov. Connally. Should we take the report seriously?

The major flaws of the Warren report

a. Ethical: Allen Dulles fired by Jfk and rumored to be the leader of the coup d'état.
b. legal: no cross examination of witnesses.
c. factual: irrational explanations such as the magic bullet.

JFK and RFK

Fireflies On Your Palms
For Olivia

Hello my little girl
Can you be gentle
Very gentle
To fireflies on your palms
Don't squeeze them
Shake them
Or crunch them
For crunching sounds
Or for the thrill of
Luminescence
Fading away

One day my little girl
When you grow up
And grow into
Cinderella shoes
Far years away
Far like distant stars
You may become
A butterfly
A radiant one
And reminisce
Luminescent fire flies
You now hold on you palms

Ch. 6:
The Journey of Private Dinkins

The story of Eugene Dinkins may also be a helpful piece in this complex crime by invisible influence.

The similarities between Lee Oswald and Eugene Dinkins – military background, young age and cues of a frame up – are remarkable and stand out.

On November 6, 1963, Pfc. Dinkins, a cryptographic code operator stationed in Metz, France, appeared in the press room of the United Nations in Geneva, Switzerland, to warn of a plot to assassinate President John F. Kennedy.

Dinkins was highly specific about his assertion with references to the timing (late November), location (Dallas) and the frame up (of a communist with Russian ties). By registered mail, Dinkins had attempted to inform the Attorney General, Robert Kennedy. He would also inform Mr. Cunningham, Charge dAffaires at the American Embassy in Luxembourg, Belgium, of his concerns.

On November 13, 1963 Dinkins was involuntarily committed to Walter Reed Hospital, where he would receive electroconvulsive treatment and various medications for an alleged mental breakdown. Months later, he would be declared permanently mentally disabled and discharged from the Army. He was receiving electroconvulsive treatment at Walter Reed at the time of the president's assassination.

As an isolated account, this story is both extraordinary and unnerving; but in the end, one might say perhaps this was just an odd event for a young men to get lucky with smart predictions and pay a high price for his rebellious acts.

There is another and far more disturbing possibility, of course: that Dinkins has stumbled across otherwise hidden, unobservable influences with a common objective—the death of JFK and the elimination of crucial evidence.

Making Waves For Truth

I have been praying hard
Praying and pleading
Bleeding
Praying and bleeding
Praying and yelling
Yelling for truth
Exhaling shrieks
Shrieks across the Atlantic
My plight
My voice
Lonesome voice in space
Making waves
In ocean and land
Forming clouds
Giant clouds
Watering my throat
For louder voices
Making new waves
For truth

Ch. 7:
Oswald working for the US government

There is no single, smoking gun to prove clearly and directly that Oswald worked for the US government. Yet, the cumulative evidence strongly points in the direction of his having been a rather good spy.

Oswald's profile is a good match for an American "James Bond". I would consider it very unlikely for a young and supposedly troubled young man from New Orleans, Louisiana, to be fluent in Russian and Spanish.

And when and how did he learn to speak Russian so well that, when he first met Marina, his future wife, who was Russian, she thought that he was Russian, too? Oswald's fluency in Russian was a credit to his language training.

Let us also remember that this was a time of extreme tension between the US and the Soviet Union. So how could Oswald manage to get in and out of the Soviet Union so easily and so fast? How could Oswald obtain a passport – with travel expenses paid by the US Department of State – after having renounced his American citizenship?

The paper trail of Oswald's covert function for the US government can be supported by two independent documents. One is a medical certificate confirming that he had contracted gonorrhea while he was stationed in Japan, but that it was in the performance his duties!

In plain English, this means he was a spy, who was having sex to gather information. Oswald worked as a radar operator at the Atsugi airbase in Japan, the home of U-2 top-secret flights across the Soviet Union. This means he must have had a high security clearance.

- Military education with fluency in Russian.
- Radar operator in Atsugi Air Base in Japan with high security clearance.
- Easy entry and fast exit from Soviet Union. Easy re-entry to U.S.A. after denouncing citizenship.
- Paper trail as an official asset to the FBI.
- Military top secret ID identical to Gary Powers, the U-2 pilot.
- Medical records consistent with medical treatment for venereal disease during military action in Japan.

Who is the King?

Who is the King?
Who is in charge?
In universe
On earth, moon
Saturn, Jupiter or Pluto?
Who is my Lord?
Who is the mother of all
Kings?
Chinese Ethiopian
Ancient Mesopotamians
Traveling Through Bosporus
To Venice
Woodcarving merchants
Gunpowder mercenaries
Truck drivers foot soldiers

Luckily I met the king
During one of my trials
In Abingdon Virginia
Trails of life through history
And asked
What makes you my king
What's your power
Your precise properties of
infinite supremacy
The king smiled
Gently patting my brain
Come close to me he whis-
pered
No much closer my boy
Much closer sit on my lap my
baby boy
Don't be afraid … let your
body free
Let your soul rest
Before I tell you
I am your King
Ever since I met your mother
Nature

Ch. 8:

Why did Fritz look away when Ruby shot Oswald?

We are all animals with mammalian genes. This means we all tend to respond to alarming events the same way. We respond. We react. We don't think. Our arms, legs and other body parts behave in unison to sudden cues of external threats. It's call "the body posture of fight or flight."

Bang! Oswald's wince, a policeman's yell (at Ruby), "You son of a bitch, Jack!", all coincided with his shooting Oswald.

Now watch the photos and observe Capt. Will Fritz, the homicide detective who had interrogated Oswald. Fritz looks entirely too calm, even oblivious in the midst of mayhem. A police detective on flight. But why?

The unnatural reaction of Capt. Fritz

Understandably, his behavior alone does not suggest wrongdoing. But is this not an easily observable piece of evidence of crucial importance? We therefore ask, Is there any other evidence of wrongdoing by Capt. Fritz in the investigation of JFK's death? A major fact is an obvious one: Lee Harvey Oswald, a high profile prisoner under the protective watch of Capt. Fritz and his men was shot. And the shooting occurred after several advance warnings of an assassination. Not to digress, but it's impossible not to recall Eugene Dinkins predictions about the fate of JFK.

The role of Jack Ruby

In this case, Ruby the killer did not hold a press conference to declare Oswald's death. He was more subtle. Impersonating a member of a vigilante group, he broadcast the details of his own planned actions .Furthermore, in the early morning hours, Ruby would call to ensure that Capt. Fritz had indeed received his messages.

All we know, in retrospect Capt. Fritz was not surprised when Ruby killed Oswald. And that's what the photos illustrate.

Other signs of Fritz' complicity

Capt. Fritz made a few more blunders with plenty of paper-trail evidence of criminal negligence. The wrongful identification of the alleged murder weapon is one of them. The obvious problem is not simply that after the initial declaration of the weapon as a Mauser, it inexplicably become a Mannlicher-Carcano, but rather that Capt. Fritz never bothered to offer am explanation for the change.

The subject of Capt. Fritz not having tape-recorded his lengthy interrogations of Oswald has received plenty of attention. This is criminal negligence. So in essence the photographs express an inner voice—the invisible voice of Capt. Fritz. They tell us that he was an active participant in the cover-up.

Summary

Oswald was killed under the watch of Capt. Fritz and his men despite ominous warnings. Capt. Fritz interrogated Oswald, but failed to keep an audio recording.

Capt. Fritz declared Oswald guilty of a crime he had not committed not long after JFK had been killed. He dismissed the sworn affidavits declaring the murder weapon a Mauser for no apparent reason.

You decide whether he was or was not guilty of criminal negligence in the death of Oswald.

A good brother

Who?
Who is?
Who is good?
Say
A man
A good man
A brother
Who, why, how?
From what kingdom, class, tribe, family, genus, species
From Ararat to Houstonian lands, soils, and oceans
Bitter not under siege
Building buildings bridges
Exploring oil, paintings
Quantum discoveries
Healing wounds and wars
Compassion not words
Action and grace
Yes grace
Grace is you
You the man
You
A brother
A great man.

Ch. 9:
The Impossible Job of Chief Justice Warren

The lives of JFK, Oswald , Ruby and Chief Justice Warren are inextricably intertwined. Their place in history and in particular in American history is sculpted by their actions and inactions.

One of the simplest ways we can observe that integration is through the supreme arbiter of mankind, which has such a profound impact on human destiny: studying the words and actions they expressed in crucial times.

JFK elegantly showed this principle when he signed National Security Action Memorandum 263 (NSAM 263), disengaging the US from involvement in Vietnam. Many believe he died because of NSAM 263 and his precise orders to discontinue the US. Military engagement in Vietnam.

Was it a coincidence that President Johnson signed NSAM 273, which reversed JFK's presidential orders, and declaring war in Vietnam only four days after the his predecessor's death?

Oswald was loyal to the end

We don't exactly know what his assignment may have been, but once arrested, Oswald knew he had been set up and was "a patsy." Yet, he never betrayed his mission or his superiors. The records show he frantically called his bosses at the CIA field offices in the Outer Banks of North Carolina. He got no response.

It would be fair to say that Jack Ruby was a reluctant assassin. He tried to save Oswald by giving advance warnings in the hope that his transfer would be called off. They did not succeed.

The conversation between Ruby and Chief Justice Warren is informative. It offers insights into the minds and hearts of Ruby and the Chief Justice under duress.

Warren/Ruby dialogue

Ruby: You you request me to go back to Washington right now, that couldn't be done could it?

Warren: No, it could not be done. That are a good many things involved in that, Mr. Ruby.

Ruby: Gentleman, my life is in danger here. You said you have the power to do what you want to do. Is that correct?

Warren: Exactly.

Ruby: Without any limitations?

Warren: Within the purview of the executive order which established the commission. We have the right to take testimony of anyone we want in this whole situation, and we have the right, if we so choose to do it, to verify that statement in any way that we wish to do it.

Ruby: But you don't have the right to take your prisoner back with you when you want to?

Warren: No, we have the power to subpoena witnesses to Washington if we want to do, but we have taken the testimony of 200 or 300 people, I would imagine, here in Dallas without going to Washington.

Ruby: Yes, but those people aren't Jack Ruby. Maybe something can be saved, something can be done. What have you got to answer to that Chief Justice Warren? I want to tell the truth and I cannot tell it here. I cannot tell it here. Now maybe certain people don't want to know the truth that may come out of me. Is that right? You can get more out of me. Let's not break up so soon. Is there any way to get me to Washington?

Warren: I beg your pardon?

Ruby: Is there any way all you getting me to Washington?

Warren: I don't know of any. I will be glad to talk to your counsel about what the situation is, Mr. Ruby, when we get an opportunity to talk.

Ruby: I will like to request that I go to Washington and you take all the tests that I have to take. It is very important. Gentleman you get into Washington you can get a fair shake out of me. If you understand the by way of talking, you have got to get me to Washington to get the tests. Gentlemen, if you want to get any further testimony, you will have to get me to Washington soon because of this something to do with future for. Where are you going back to Washington?

What does it mean?

For the record, it is important to know that the Chief Justice had the authority to transfer Ruby to Washington DC. In order to understand the statements by the Chief Justice, it is imperative to know of what he had been told by President Lyndon Johnson. During a conversation (which was recorded and has been preserved), the president had suggested that Oswald must be found guilty to prevent a potential nuclear war with the Soviet Union.

It is reasonable to infer that bringing Ruby to Washington would have complicated arriving at the predetermined guilt of Oswald as "the lone assassin". And on one level this may explain the stonewalling by the Chief Justice.

There is also top-secret information of which the Warren Commission had been informed—that Lee Harvey Oswald was working as an informant for the FBI, with specific paper trail of monies paid to him, including his income tax forms — that burdened the Chief Justice.

A psychological assessment

From a psychological perspective, the Chief Justice was not only misled by President Johnson but was also faced with the potentially serious and embarrassing exposure of the FBI's entanglement in the assassination of JFK. This was an historically challenging time for the country.

This was also a daunting task for the Chief Justice of the United States. The nation was grieving. People wanted to know the truth, but another truth was saving face, protecting order and the nation's honor lest the United States be regarded as another "banana republic".

Within the Warren Commission, Allen Dulles, the former Director of the CIA whom JFK had retired, was masterful in clever manipulations to mislead the committee. A transparent example of a dirty trick by Dulles was reported by Matthew Smith, in JFK: THE SECOND PLOT, a book circulated among the committee's members, alleging that, historically, American assassin's had been mentally impaired individuals, disturbed souls like Lee Harvey Oswald.

Should the Chief Justice be faulted?

Should the Chief Justice be faulted for the membership of the committee? No, because President Johnson hand-picked them. Of course, the Chairman's job was not to second-guess the integrity of its members. Nor was it to question President Johnson, who had bluntly and repeatedly hinted at a nuclear confrontation with the Soviet Union (with specific projected casualties of some 40 million Americans).

Many of those influences created an atmosphere in which, not facts but fear, catastrophic possibilities and the bullying by President Johnson predetermined the final outcome. This is not to defend the Chief Justice but to explain the complex framework he was operating within. His inaction had a profoundly negative impact on the events that followed. What might have occurred had Ruby been allowed to tell? What Ruby knew must have been combustible. The next chapter on premature deaths may reveal a few cues.

55

Salutation

The inferno in me
Neither red nor black
The kindling
Not fading nor raging
Speechless I stand
By battles lost
Battles long
People loved
Friends gone
No farewells
No tears
Ashes warm

Trumpets will mourn
Friends gone
Damaged limbs
Trees branches
Giant roots
Is war over
Limbs under bridge
Does it matter who won
My Inferno
Will be gone
When I am gone
Today
I stand up alone
Saluting
My friends
Ashes warm
Rekindling memories

Ch. 10:
Premature deaths of witnesses and reporters

People ask: how could many crimes have remained secrets and not surfaced for 50 years?

It is true that suppressing the truth in America may be more difficult than some other places, yet it is also clear that the sudden disappearance of crucial voices not only delayed the discovery of the facts but had a chilling impact on others interested in pursuing the truth.

Below is a short and incomplete list of witnesses, reporters and investigators who died suddenly or prematurely or under suspicious circumstances.

The premature deaths:

1. Lee Harvey Oswald (undercover)
2. Jack Ruby (FBI asset)*
3. Robert Kennedy (Atty. Gen.)
4. John Kennedy, Jr. (reporter)
5. Dorothy Kilgallen (reporter)
6. C D jackson (reporter)*
7. Paul Mandel (reporter)*
8. Hank Suydam (reporter)*
9. Lou Staples (reporter)
10. Bill Hunter (reporter)
11. James Koethy (reporter)
12. James Altgens (reporter)

13. Gary Underhill (CIA agent)
14. William Colby (CIA chief)
15. William Sullivan (FBI assistant director)
16. Louis Nichols (FBI number three man)*
17. James Cadigan (FBI document expert)
18. JM English (FBI forensics)*
19. General Earl Wheeler
20. Roger Craig (Dallas policeman)
21. Hiram Ingram (Dallas policeman)*
22. James Chaney (Dallas policeman)*
22. Bill Decker (Dallas policeman)
23. Frank Martin (Dallas policeman)*
24. E R Walthers (Dallas policeman)
25. Dr. Nicholas Chetta (pathologist)
26. Dr. James Weston (pathologist)
27. Dr. Mary Sherman
28. William Pritzer (Navy autopsy photographer)
30. Congressman Hale Boggs (Warren Commission)
31 Thomas Howard (attorney)*
32. Earl Smith (friend of Dorothy Killgallen)
33. Henry Delaune (brother-in-law of Dr. Chetta)
34. Dr. John Holbrook (Ruby psychiatrist)*
35. Clayton Fowler (Ruby attorney)*

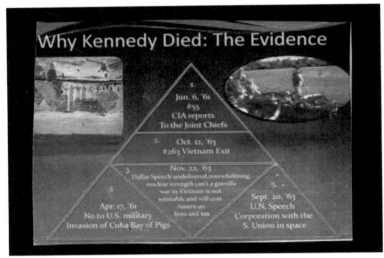

This list represents data gathered from public records and JFK related research presented in the bibliography. The sudden fatalities caused by man-made actions (suicide or homicide) or by alleged "accidents" have been included. Fatalities from suspicious and rapid progressive medical conditions have also been included but are marked with an asterisk (*). Here they are sorted by categories:

Early deaths	number of deaths
Law enforcement	13
Reporters :	7
Doctors:	4
Attorneys :	3
Armed forces:	2
Congressman:	1

Jack Ruby associated premature deaths

Attorneys	2
Reporters	3
Psychiatrist	1
Self	1

An Ass And A Fox

On an empty bus
Going nowhere
Idling engine
A bus passes by
Then a lion
And two donkeys
Arguing about
Hard labor
Not enough food
Bad bosses
Inflation
Rude young asses
Dogs barking too much

"Hey driver
Can we go already"
"Yes sir" the driver says
"You're the boss
Tell me where to go"
"I'd love to see the White House
Or Lincoln Memorial"
"Give me a bigger challenge"
the driver says
"Take me to Heaven" I say
"The real one or the one man
made?"
"You decide"
"The real one is easy
All I have to do is to kill you
The one here
Perhaps difficult
You need a passport
And you have none
For you're an ass
And this is a fox jungle"

Ch. 11:
Are we observing cerebro-genocide?

Death is influential. This death has been as influential since November 22, 1963 as if it had occurred 10,000 years ago.

Would it be an over-reaction to view the possible man-made demise of 35 people—including nine reporters, four doctors, a congressman, a former Attorney General and several civil servants—with the duty to protect the Constitution—as (what might be called) "cerebro-genocide"? What then is cerebro-genocide? The organized killings of intellectuals who are, in this case, witnesses to, reporting about or investigating a crime.

The term "cerebro-genocide" may or may not be applicable to the killings of American intelligentsia associated with JFK's death. But what other term could be more appropriate to describe the tragedy?

It has happened before

This is not a new phenomenon. The 20th century witnessed the mass murders of Turkish intellectuals of Armenian heritage, German intellectuals of Jewish background and Western-friendly Cambodians experienced holocausts and genocides. The observation that a large number of American intellectuals have fallen victim to unnatural death is a depressing truth.

What should we call this phenomenon, if not "cerebro-genocide"? Mass cerebro-homicide? or intelligent homicide? For obvious reasons, the silencing process is very well-designed and executed. The measures taken to ensure its complex and destructive aim also includes methods to conceal the criminal act by misleading the authorities with intelligent and phantom traps.

By the time the entanglements surface, for all practical purposes, the criminal act becomes an ancient irrelevant intellectual statistic. The goal is accomplished. The secret is buried. The message is delivered: telling the truth is risking your life.

Organized killing of intelligensia

The organized killing of intelligentsia observed in the 20th century was performed quietly but effectively and openly. There is no evidence to suggest that intelligent effort was built into the killings of intelligentsia to keep them secret. But times have changed so has the intelligent design of criminal conduct in the second half of the 20th century.

The playbook of JFK's death illustrates a few of the essentials, the basic principles of modern intelligent homicide. Do horrible things but cover them up by plausible deniability. And this means no apparent links between the victims and the criminal architects.

In the spirit of justice and scientific integrity we can state that good many people did die because of intellectual courage and their pursuit of the truth. The evidence suggests that none of these deaths were accidental.

The list here is conservative

For instance, the list presented in this chapter is conservative and does not include the great many sudden deaths of numerous innocent witnesses:

William W Whaley, the cab driver who gave Oswald his final taxi ride; Lee Bowers, the man in the railroad tower behind Dealey Plaza; Rose Cheramie and Karyn Kupicinet, both of whom predicted JFK's death before November 22, also met premature deaths.

Perhaps small time criminals with Mafia ties had something to do with those unfortunate killings but they cannot explain the catastrophic demise of the American intelligentsia .

Noteworthy has been the ominous timing of many of the killings. John Kennedy, Jr., Dorothy Kilgallen and Lou Staples were victimized soon after making public statements of intent to further investigate or publish about the assassination.

Some especially interesting cases

All six Dallas policemen who perished had made public statements contradictory to the misrepresentations by the Dallas Police Department. The evidence is also consistent that Ruby/Oswald associates were possibly eliminated.

Howard and Fowler both attorneys for Jack Ruby, the Ruby forensic psychiatrist, and all three reporters with access to Ruby died of unnatural or premature reasons.

William Sullivan, the FBI's Number Two man, was killed in a bizarre hunting accident prior to his scheduled testimony before the Senate intelligence committee. Gary Underhill, a CIA agent, even predicted his own death by gunshot wounds to his head.

In essence, there is apparent mathematical certainty of the conclusion that many intellectuals with crucial information about JFK's death were silenced. And that may be the sad but correct answer to, "How could such serious criminal actions have remained secrets for more than 50 years?"

JFK

A man of honor
An Armenian King
An Irish Anna Frank
The man who said no
To second Nagasaki
An unusual man
A Pakistani Catholic who
Flew to Massachusetts
From Great Britain
Aware of witch hunts
Remnants of ignorance
Yet a man
An unusual man

Ch. 12:
Oswald did not kill JFK

Complexity or no complexity, the evidence is sufficiently abundant and compelling to exonerate Oswald: He was not the lone killer of JFK.

Equally compelling is the evidence that Oswald had worked for the Armed Forces and at the time of his death he had become an informant for the FBI.

In view of overwhelming proof of Oswald's innocence, the request so eloquently expressed by his own mother for Oswald to rest at the Arlington National Cemetery deserves public debate and national attention.

Jackie

Like An Apple In An Orchard

Where life begins
Where it ends
Are you confused my friend
Confused
Like an apple
Like an apple in an orchard
Living or a nonliving thing

Do forests feel
Do tanks sense
Do bullets sob
Is virus a living
Why not my memories

Who is kind who is coward
Who is reckless or daring
An apple once living
May fall prey to masters
Maestros of lies and liars
Aren't we all like apples

Empathy for an apple
May come from a sudden fall
Sudden and earthshaking
You may not mind
Being eaten
Eaten alive
Even thanking the mouth
Thanking a lot
Your new host
Your new home

Ch. 13:

The sad news about Greer, Kellerman and Roberts

Since its inception in 1865, **the Secret Service** has been part of the history of the White House and the US presidents. Not only it's enormously complex and thankless job, but its rare failings have become the signature trait of the organization in collective memory.

The following observations are not about the past for the future of the Secret Service. Nor it is about the infinite data of crucial decisions prior to the presidents visit Dallas Texas. It is about the actions of Greer, Kellerman and Roberts right before, during, and after JFK assassination.

Highly distinguished researchers, Vincent M. Palamara and Philip H. Melanson, and their scholarly contributions may provide any reader with comprehensive information about the Secret Service and its conduct during JFK's Dallas visit. My observations will be limited to the specific times and people identified above.

10 mistakes by 3 secret service men:

Mistake #1: topless car, hostile environment.
Responsible agent: Emory Roberts

To say that the visit to Dallas had associated risks for his JFK's safety is virtually too obvious to state. A week earlier, Adlai Stevenson had been struck on the head during a Dallas appearance. Death threats against JFK had been received or intercepted by the FBI and the Secret Service. (Rumors of JFK having ordered the removal of the bubble top have long-since been refuted.)

Mistake #2: leaving two agents behind
Responsible agent: Emory Roberts

JFK without a bodyguard? The president without immediate protection?

Special Agent Hank Rybka and his partner were both ordered to remain at Love Field by Roberts. Rybka was more than surprised by the orders—he was dumbfounded and dismayed.

Mistake #3: unsafe travel route with two 90° turns
Responsible agent: Forrest Sorrells

The travel route was in direct violation of the Secret Service guidelines, which did not allow travel slower than 25 mph and 90° turns.

Mistake #4: refusal to receive assistance from the US Army 12th military intelligence group
Responsible agent: unknown

The offer to help with presidential protection by the U.S. Army's 12th Military Intelligence Group stationed in Dallas was turned down.

Mistake #5: failure to clear rooftops bridges and high risk spots
Responsible agent: Forrest Sorrels

Mistake #6: no response to hostile threats
Responsible agent: Roy Kellerman

Unsafe travel route with two 90° turns against the Secret Service guidelines

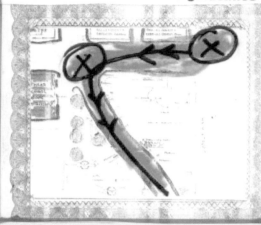

The U.S. Army's 12th Military Intelligence Group, stationed in Dallas, offered help for extra protection before JFK's Dallas trip.

The Secret Service said, No! No! No!

An open umbrella on a bright day, a person with a black object waving yet no response from Kellerman. Why?

No response to hostile threats:
an open umbrella on a rainless day.

Mistake #7: no attempt to protect the president during gunfire
Responsible agent: Roy Kellerman

The gunfire lasted some nine or ten seconds. No attempt was made to offer protective cover for the President and others. Instead Kellerman was observed talking on the radio.

Mistake #8: no attempt to fire back
Responsible agent: Roy Kellerman

For the duration of the attack, the presidential limousine was peppered by gunfire with no attempt to fire back by Kellerman or others from the Secret Service.

Mistake #9: deceleration during gunfire
Responsible agent: William Greer

Instead of acceleration out of Dealey Plaza at the first sign of trouble, William Greer brought the presidential limousine to a complete stop before speeding away. This made JFK a perfect target. In addition to numerous witness reports confirming that the limo had stopped during the gunfire, the actions of agent Clint Hill support deceleration by Greer. From 20 feet behind the Lincoln, Agent Hill would not have been able to catch up with the presidential limousine to help Mrs. Kennedy.

The methodical documentation by Vince Palamara of the witnesses at the Dealey Plaza is of importance to further support deceleration by Greer. For instance "*Newsweek*" (12/2/1963), p. 2 reported: "for a chaotic moment" the limousine "ground to an uncertain halt." Another reporter, Bo Byers, observed "the presidential limousine almost came to a stop, a dead stop." (C-SPAN 11/10/1993). NBC reporter, Robert MacNeill, said, "The driver slammed on the brakes" (WF AA – ABC 11/22/1963). Credit to further documentation by Vince Palamara has been the confirmation by 10 Dallas city police officers individually and collectively validating what has been established: the presidential limousine came to a halt during the shooting.

Mistake #10 : washing off the crime scene evidence
Responsible agent: Roy Kellerman

Captured by photographic evidence, an agent washing off crime scene evidence was a criminal act with the apparent motive to get rid of crucial forensic evidence. Regardless of the motive, it was a major blunder.

Rushing Rusty To Foreign Lands

Pardon me
My Lord
From War Virginia
I holler
Could I trust the old man
Is my father a good man
Unlike my uncle
My uncle Sam
A bad apple never caught
Not a day in prison

My Lord
My uncle did Vietnam
After killing JFK
And more horrors
Bad lies I reckon
Arms of mass destruction
Rushing Rusty to foreign lands
Before wasting baby young

My Lord
I'm poor and poorly read
May I burden you more
Trust is gold my Lord
Tell me straight my Lord
Is my father an honest man
Is he unlike my uncle
If Rusty died for reason

Ch. 14:
What the Secret Service tells us

Observing Secret Service contributions to the death of JFK is easy because of their transparency. Sadly beyond the top 10 mistakes, there were many others. The point here is not to bash the Secret Service but convey a sense that betrayal and deception by Kellerman, Greer and Roberts were crucial to the success of the assassination.

Even without the specific documentation of many other errors – the kidnapping of the president's body, the disappearance of bullet fragments retrieved during the autopsy, the loss of JFK's brain and misrepresentations by Kellerman and Greer during their testimony before the Warren commission – their failures seem both serious and tragic.

This brings us back to the topic of complexity and how a single or a few errors in complex systems may trigger catastrophic outcome. In complex systems, the rules are different.

Back to COMPLEXITY again

COMPLEXITY by Melanie Mitchell is my favorite book on this topic. Her remarkable study begins with the observation of ant colonies and their enormous collective intelligence as little living things that can build very sophisticated structures or ravage large forests. Everything is teamwork.

What a single unit does or fails to do impacts the rest of the team. Collectively teamwork can create brilliance or invite disaster by tiny errors. This is where Greer's stopping the car in the middle of gunfire is not simply a minor mishap. It is an invitation for disaster.

This is where Roberts' orders to keep Rybka off the motorcade suddenly gains new meaning. Zero instant protection. This is where we can judge Kellerman's preoccupation with his radio and failure to offer any help to JFK as lethal.

Neither the single act of a Secret Service agent by itself—nor the work of a single ant—seems significant, yet in concert with other tiny forces they could destroy with devastating power and efficiency. And this is the essence of the case against Greer, Kellerman and Roberts.

Lessons to be learned

One of the most difficult challenges of complex crimes is it's intelligent immunity to our current legal system . For our system is built upon observable evidence and linear logic.

Complex crimes, after all, involve intelligent deception to mislead the legal system. The more sophisticated the criminals, the more inadequate the legal system to catch them. It's a reasonable assumption that the masterminds of JFKs death were intelligent minds who appreciated the weaknesses of our system.

They understood, for instance, the importance of visual evidence. They reengineered the movies and the photos to cover-up Greer stopping the car. By selectively editing the film, they also managed to project the appearance that everything happened very fast and there was no time for the secret service agents to help the president

The importance of the limo stop

Nothing could be further removed from the reality of the assassination. Nine seconds is a very long time—and some, such as James Fetzer, contend that it may have been 20 to 30 seconds long. It's plenty of time for Kellerman to have provided cover and shield the president from the bullet shower.

Here is the bottom line to remember. Nine seconds or more: no attempt to shield. But the masterminds outsmarted us by visual illusions of shrinking the assassination to a few seconds—with no stoppage—and with plenty of heroics by Clint Hill.

The urgent need to upgrade our judicial system with intelligent systems to recognize, monitor and—most importantly—detect complex crimes is our collective challenge. I don't believe there is any American or a rational human being who would condone a system in which an American president is killed by criminal methods to further empower other equally intelligent systems to ensure its complicity half a century later.

Lions Flirting With Lambs

One day
Not that far in the future
Birds will swim
Fish will fly to freedom
Men not start wars
All women playing soccer
Dolphins friends with lions
Lions flirting with lambs
For friendship
And on that day that very night
The blue moon shall laugh
Laughing hard
Shaking earth so hard
A new world will be born
A world
A beautiful world
Beautiful fireworks
Firecrackers
Radiating joy
That will be
My fourth of July

Ch. 15:
The sad truth about the Zapruder film

It's been called the most famous documentary movie in history, and the mythology that has grown up around it is widely known. A women's clothing manufacturer, Abraham Zapruder, decided to film the president's visit to Dallas on November 22, 1963.

His office was close to the presidential motorcade, an event that would give him a chance to use his new Bell and Howell 8mm movie camera. From his vantage point atop the grassy knoll on the north side of Elm Street he would take 27 seconds of film at 18.3 frames per second that would show in remarkable (or, better, gruesome) detail John F. Kennedy's getting shot dead in broad daylight.

Rules of brain functioning

The first step toward understanding the film is to understand some of the basic rules of human brain function.

First, 18th of a second is too fast for your brain to process in formation. Images shown at that speed, no matter how irrational they might be, can be made to look perfectly normal. They are simply moving too fast for your brain to differentiate absurdity from reality or alteration from authenticity.

The prefrontal cortex, the brain's processing center, cannot synthesize, analyze and form conclusions about individual images if they are streaming past it every18th of a second. As a result becomes possible to fool a lot of the people a lot of the time. And this is precisely why even a very intelligent and visually sophisticated person is very likely to miss the obvious inconsistencies of the film.

When we slow down and study the images one by one, the forgeries become visible. The natural reaction is disbelief. "No, this is not possible." This kind of obvious alteration must have been discovered immediately. It could not have been unrecognized for half a century

Slowing down the film

Or so the story goes. It's an easy story to believe – seductive in its simplicity, fascinating in its improbability, compelling in its results. Like the story, the film itself is easy to take at face value. Viewed at normal speed, it unfolds with smooth precision from its seemingly ordinary beginning to its horrifying end.

Watching it, it's easy to forget that each second of seamless motion is actually made up of 18 separate frames of film. Look at each frame individually, and the film takes on an entirely different character. Irrational images are everywhere, beginning with the very first frame, which shows buildings where there aren't supposed to be.

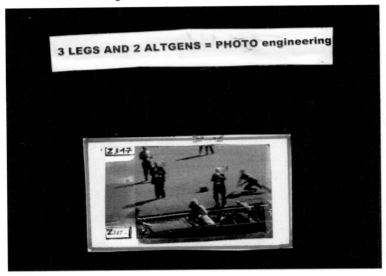

In that frame, the image of the intersection of Houston and Elm is distorted—almost surreal—dominated by a building that is not even located on the intersection. The Purse Building is actually 100 yards or more away, yet looks as if it has been dragged down the street to a new address. But in the Zapruder film, reality has been altered and everything is out of whack.

Evidence of Alteration: #277 BrehmJr is invisible; by #286, 9 frames and ½ a second later he is not only standing up by his father but has a shadow and hands ready to clap.

Zapruder #277

Zapruder #286

The same is true of the rest of the movie. People grow and shrink. They shed limbs. The turn of the head or the motion of a limousine can play out in ways that are physically impossible. For an excellent analysis of the film, see Jim Fetzer's *THE GREAT ZAPRUDER FILM HOAX* (2003).

Abraham Zapruder may have had honorable intentions filming the JFK motorcade in Dallas. What the evidence shows with clarity is that the available version of the film was revised to mislead the public. That the revision of the movie has fooled the world for almost half a century is a credit to the Machiavellian ingenuity with which it was done.

Reversed sequencing of Zapruder frames 344-354.
By 354 M. Summers seems relaxed. The reality: M. Summers jumped up and ran in response to gunfire

344 M. Summers

346

348

351

353

354

Because of the reversal of the frames, the correct sequence starts with 354 then 353 then 351 and continues in reverse to 344.

America America

For Jim Fetzer

In love with different parts
Different towns
Distant lands
Freedom and democracy
We do cherish the dream

Then waking up
Questioning the dream
Can we talk and walk the dream
Should we dream just a dream
Should we wake up to the chill
The chill of mourning something
Can't quite tell the missing
The magic of great dreams

Let us keep dreaming
Wake up America
America America
Land of dreamers
Me too dreaming
Going to the moon
Walking on the moon
The magic of dreaming

Ch. 16:
The Sad Truth about James "Ike" Altgens

James "Ike" Altgens name is synonymous with Dealey Plaza and with November 22, 1963. This army veteran, an accomplished Second World War photographer, became a legend for the images he captured in Dealey Plaza. His achievements were extraordinary. He managed to take photographs on three different streets, first catching the presidential limo on Main, then continuing to take photos on Houston and Em streets. He even managed to photograph Clinton Hill's heroic climb onto the presidential limo to assist Jackie Kennedy.

My curiosity of Altgens was aroused by his sudden death. He and his wife died together of carbon monoxide poisoning. And because I had been sensitized to the sudden demise of many people associated with JFK's death, I wondered about the possibility of a foul play.

My curiosity urged me to travel to Dallas and follow the path of Altgens on November 22. What you will observe are the photos from this fascinating journey.

Questions about Altgen photos:

1. How many JFKs can be seen in the photo on the next page?

2. Is it possible to view his head through a back view mirror?

3. Why do people show such different facial and body responses?

4. Why is Greer turned all the way around and holding a black object?

5. Why can't we see Kellerman face but we can see Gov. Connally?

6. Is Mrs. Kennedy holding on to JFK's arm?

7. Did Altgens take all the photos, one on Main Street, another on Houston and more on Elm Street?

8. Did Mr. and Mrs. Altgens die together accidentally of carbon monoxide poisoning?

9. Did Altgens ever notice there were two side-by-side images of him in Zapruder frame number 230?

Answers to those questions:

1. Watch the arrow. A second JFK silhouette?

2. The back view mirror should block JFK. It doesn't.

3. Central smiling women, agents alarmed looking back, the policeman on alert contradict each other. Crowd reactions tend to be in unison with body responses identical to each other. Simply put, if shots were being fired, those women would not be smiling.

4. Is it a weapon?

5. Unlikely.

6. Can't be Mrs. Kennedy's hand. Too big. Furthermore, her bracelet was thin.

7. Unlikely. Two photos are possible. Not three. I tried to imitate his run wouldn't come close to it.

8. Suspicious.

9. Unlikely.

The Turtle Said

The turtle said
"You stallion
You so huge
Such a horse"
And the horse said
'You are short
And scared too
not know what life is
Always scared hiding"
I intervened of course
"Let's make peace
No name-calling
We all living things
Let's hold hands
And pray
Thank God for life"
An instant before
Horse kicking me hard
Landing me on neighbor's roof
For the neighbor yell
"You nothing, you enabler
Made a good horse kick"
And that's when
The turtle spoke up
"Don't forget Sir
We are all savages
Dressed as animals"

Ch. 17:
Photo-psychology: the crucial moment

This photo is very informative. It is the smoking gun of photo engineering consistent with the not so easily observable psychological cues concealed in the image.

Watch the faces of the smiling women on the left side. Also watch the body reactions of the secret servicemen and James Chaney, the motorcycle policeman. Also watch JFK clutching his throat. In this nano second, JFK has already been shot with loud bangs of gunfire. We also know that governor Connally was loud and yelling.

This is a crisis moment. A noisy startling event. It is simply impossible for the women to be laughing or smiling. It is equally unlikely for the Secret Service men in the follow-up car to look straight as if nothing were going on when other agents are alarmed. Almost always, crowd responses share a common vector with people in concert turning toward the perceived location of danger.

This photo shows an image of several Secret Service agents—as if handicapped by attention deficit disorder—in Dealey Plaza on November 22, 1963.

Altgens claimed he ran from the corner of Houston and Main streets (Point A) to Ellen Street across from the Stemmons sign (Point B). He managed to capture the presidential limo some 40 feet away from the Stemmons sign opened the premises (Point D). He had already captured the limo on Houston Street (Point C). This suggests he ran faster from Point A to Point B then the limo traveling from Point C to Point D. This is an unlikely occurrence.

It would be a mistake to blame Altgens for the obvious alterations of the Dealey Plaza photos. We have no evidence that he was responsible for the reengineering . However, it is reasonable to think that he knew about the alterations. Or he knew that a few of the photographs credited to him were not his.

He never spoke up. Furthermore he never offered rational explanations as to why, after the first photo with the image of the presidential limousine on Elm Street, he did not continue taking other images of the slow death of JFK until his last shot of Jackie and Hill and the limo near the Triple Underpass. Or is it possible that he took many other pictures and they vanished?

Altgens was consistent in his explanations about the absence of many more dramatic images from Elm Street. He was stunned and temporarily froze, the veteran photographer explained. He was just too upset to take more photographs. I suppose this is not much different than for a senior neurosurgeon to be paralyzed by a bloody malignant brain tumor.

Perhaps this was true. But it was more likely that a battle tested photographer had other reasons for his failure to take the most important images imaginable for a photographer.

Along with the Z-movie, the photographic images have defined the reality of what occurred at the Daley Plaza. This is why further analysis would be of help. Let us review the basics. You have an accomplished veteran photographer with unique credentials dating back to the Second World War. He now has nine seconds to capture images of historical significance. The first photo is already history. The camera is on and ready to capture anything in sight.

That's when paralysis takes over. Total paralysis. Indecision. Or coverup?

They do not require any explanation except to say they are not believable. Obviously, Altgens heard and registered the gunfire. For sure, he heard Gov. Connally's yells and noticed the muteness of JFK. He had the perfect spot to witness the slow death of JFK over the next nine seconds.

Nine seconds is a long time. Let us count. 1-2-3-4-5-6-7-8-9 is so much time for more pictures he didn't take. He was aware of the commotion and familiar with the sounds of bullets and war. There is death and terror in the air.

These are the kinds of things that excites professionals, reporters or photographers. This may actually be a catalyst for greater creative production. In essence this is the perfect time and the perfect place to capture history and let the world watch, observe, feel the agony in Daley Plaza at 12:30 noon local time on November 22, 1963.

And then what happens? Nothing. He knew what happened to Ruby, who wanted to tell Chief Justice Warren what he knew. I suppose he was also aware of the sudden death of Dorothy Kilgallen, the NBC reporter who had proudly announced to many that she had uncovered the truth by interviewing Ruby.

Because of his location, Altgens knew Oswald was not the killer. Like most witnesses he would have known that the fatal shots came from the grassy Knoll and not from the 6th floor of Texas School Book Depository. And like millions he also watched Oswald's death. All these tragic events may explain the great photographer's long silence.

Don't Be Afraid To Dance With Me

A dreamer
I dream and dream
Dreaming of
A warm fireside chat
A chat with truth finders
Good men
Marching to a different drum
Heart brains and hard labor
"Hey mam and sir can we talk
Can we really talk frankly
Why to hunt down doves
Shooting robins
Or torment healers?
Let us hold hands
Let us find truth
Don't be shy hold my hand
Don't be afraid to dance with me
To build schools pools ships
Why not climb mountains
Catch big fish
Cook white sharks
Let fish swim
Let robins and dolphins fly"
*And in **my** dreams*
Robins and dolphins fly
By a giant fireplace
Kindness and reason aglow
We are dancing
Dancing forever
Dancing and dancing

Ch. 18:
Understanding photo-graphic re-construction

With such a wealth of images it is easy to be overwhelmed. It is easier to get lost in minute details inconsequential for solving the big puzzle. Hence to overlook the core message, the central intent of the remaking of the photographic deceptions.

To put it simply. Is that a central theme for the deception? Is the purpose is as simple as a simple coverup? Is there something more?

Friday, November 22, 1963 would be sculpted in our collective memory with a few striking images more than others. Altgens' Elm Street photos—the first one with the president clutching his throat and the Secret Service men looking at the Texas School Book Depository and the second with Clint Hill climbing onto the presidential limousine assisting Mrs. Kennedy.

The core message: dedicated Secret Service men looking at the spot from where the shots came and a hero trying to save the president. Yes, this has been the core message. And what is the truth?

Both photos are altered this means the core message is wrong as well. In fact the facts suggest that the Secret Service acts were not heroic, just the opposite they failed to protect the president. They let all of us down that day.

It would be reasonable to consider that a cover-up was also an objective for the great many alterations. To begin with, the 8 or 9 second gunfire. through the movies and photos came across as if it was virtually instantaneous. It wasn't. For bullets to bombard the presidential limousine for 8 or nine seconds and for the Secret Service men feign dumb paralysis could have only been covered up by manipulating the visual images.

The sad truth of November 22, 1963 is that there were no heroes that day. Later, when people tried to speak up, they became dead heroes and joined the list of Roger Craig, Dorothy Kilgallen and John Kennedy, Jr., whose private plane plunged into the Atlantic Ocean soon after he announced his intentions to investigate his father's death.

There is good news however. It's difficult to forever suppress the truth.

Living In The Wind

Singing in the wind
Hearing the clouds
Grass talking
Us rolling in hay
Finding pebbles
In shallow waters
Where grandpa swimming
Is he hearing what I hear
Am I Longing for childhood
Or the wind
Telling me something
Something nice
My people gone
Are not gone
Living in the wind
Missing me as much

Ch. 19:
Complexity and the Death of JFK

We have created a national delusion of "Oswald killed JFK" by highly complex methods. A modern system's ability to produce mass data of misinformation is impressive and at times overwhelming. We can observe the relation between the reality and the national delusion in the daily news of JFK's death half a century later.

The very minute and irrelevant details of Oswald's life or the actions of the Secret Service agents can become the subject of a prime time TV show, as if all the scholarly documentation about the assassination has never occurred. This itself is as sad as the denial of the Nazi Holocaust, the Armenian genocide or the atrocities committed under Stalin and Mao.

In JFK the active refusal to refer to what occurred as a controversial theory of conspiracy is grotesque.

Extraordinarily mishaps consistent with intelligent design

1. *The Christchurch Star* news prematurely reporting the president's death and Oswald's guilt.

2. An agent washing off the crime scene evidence.

3. The change of the alleged murder weapon from the Mauser to the Mannlicher-Carcano.

4. The invalid autopsy at Bethesda Naval Hospital with Dr. Humes burning medical records.

5. President Johnson telling the Chief Justice Warren of a phantom nuclear confrontation with the Soviet Union to secure an automatic guilty verdict for Oswald.

6. President Johnson asking Dr. Charles Crenshaw to obtain a death bed confession from Oswald.

7. The disappearance of the president's brain.

8. Chief Justice Warren misinforming Ruby by suggesting he lacked the authority to take Ruby to Washington DC.

9. The altered autopsy x-rays.

10. The reengineering of Zapruder and Altgens.

11. Deceleration, not acceleration, during the gunfire.

12. No attempt to shield the president during the gunfire lasting nine seconds.

13. The murders of reporters Dorothy Killgallen, James Koethy and Bill Hunter.

Did A Poison Arrow Contribute To The Final Outcome?

• The President suffered a small entry throat wound.

• A man identified as "the Cuban" seems to be pointing a gun-like object at the president at the same time of the fatal shots.

• Despite major head wounds incompatible with life the president survived 30 minutes with cardiovascular system still functional consistent with saxitoxin influence. There seems to be no plausible explanation for his 30 minute survival after massive head wounds.

- The president was immobilized and silent consistent with saxitoxin toxicity.

- Saxitoxin was available and used by CIA to neutralize large dogs according to the testimony of William Colby the CIA director.

- The above findings were presented in San Diego to the American Academy of Forensic Psychiatry in 2009 and published in *Medical Hypotheses* in 2010.

Did A Poison Arrow Help Kill Pres. Kennedy?

1. The President suffered a small entry throat wound.
2. A man identified as " the Cuban" seems to be pointing a gun like object at the president at the same time of the fatal shots.
3. Despite massive head wounds incompatible with life the president survived 30 minutes with cardiac function consistent with saxitoxin influence. There seems to be no plausible explanation for his 30 minute survival after massive head wounds.
4. The president was immobilized and silent consistent with saxitoxin toxicity.
5. Saxitoxin was available and used to neutralize large dogs according to the testimony of William Colby the CiA director.
6. The above findings were presented in San Diego at the American Academy Of Forensic Psychiatry in 2009 and published in Medical Hypotheses in 2010.

Willis photo shows the Cuban pointing a weapon like object at the president. Moments before Bronson's photo shows the Cuban was waving. These photos support the poison arrow hypotheses.

Never admit mistakes

"We should never
Never ever
Admit mistakes"
My friend Giorgio
A Sicilian mule preaches
Born in that little village
Surrounded by vineyards
That's where
Exactly where
His kind father
A gentle mule received
Dozens and dozens
Mean lashes
Ripping skin some blood
All upon
Confession in confidence
Behind thick walls
"Yes I did kick this short ape
Masquerading doctor
Squeezing my colonies"

Papa Georgio had barked
Cried and begged for mercy
The ape went on till….
Rumors of a bloodied vet
Pancaked and down
Engulfing entire village
Rising anger
Waving whips and wisdom
"Never admit wrongdoing"
Inherited by
My friend George
Now a preacher
In that village
Not far from Washington
That's why
We would never admit
JFK's death was an inside job

Ch. 20:
Treason from the Inside

Madeleine Duncan Brown, long-term mistress of Lyndon Johnson, made headlines in British tabloids by claiming that LBJ knew in advance of President Kennedy's death. She repeated the same story many

times. Her stories made waves but received only limited attention from students of his assassination.

An interesting document from NSO that seems to confirm what Ms. Brown stated half a century ago. Circulated among top government executives, including LBJ, the day before assassination declared the news of JFK getting shot.

Eerily, this is too reminiscent of Oliver Stone's movie and the reality that before the president died the news of his death were published in New Zealand. The president died at 1 PM Texas time (7 AM New Zealand time) and by then the newspapers were giving the details of the assassination with more details about Oswald's background.

The Christchurch newspaper article and this NSA document bring credibility to Madeleine Brown and her conviction that LBJ was an insider in JFK's death.

The evidence of conspiracy by Lyndon and other administration insiders includes:

- NSO memo of 11/21/1963 announcing the presidents death one day before it occurred;

- *Christchurch Star news* announcing the President's death and Oswald's guilt before the President died;

- the reengineering of the Zapruder movie and of James Altgens (AP) photographs of the ambush at Dealey Plaza;

- invalid postmortem examination and altered x-rays of The president at Bethesda Naval Hospital.

McNamara and Bundy

JFK's top aides, Robert McNamara, Secretary of Defense, and McGeorge Bundy, his national security advisor, did not speak to one another after 1996, when McNamara's IN RETROSPECT became a national bestseller.

What offended Bundy about IN RETROSPECT?

McNamara blamed Bundy indirectly, quietly displaying the obvious treason by Bundy aides to undermine the president's policy of disengagement in Vietnam. He documented the treacheries by Hilsman and Forestall to authorize a coup d'etat in Vietnam and the assassination of Diem brothers in violation of JFK's orders.

McNamara portrayed himself as a reluctant participant in the death of JFK, placing the blame on Bundy and others who orchestrated the Honolulu meeting the day before his assassination.

McNamara's IN RETROSPECT is a tragic treasure of American history. We should cry of learning the truth and be thankful that McNamara had the courage to report the facts. The book makes it easy to understand why Bundy stopped talking to McNamara after 1996.

McGeorge Bundy's Role

Water flows down a hill, heat travels from hot to cold and the second law of thermodynamics suggests Bundy was instrumental in the assassination of our 35th president John F Kennedy.

Consistent with the second law of thermodynamics all processes have a direction in life and the sum of Bundy treacheries contributions. Consider the following:

— the reversal of JFK's orders of air support for rebels at Bay of Pigs;

— the cable of August 27, 1963, to Ambassador Lodge green-lighting a coup d'état in Vietnam;

— the personal note from his assistant Hillman to Lodge to authorize the coup d'état;

— keeping General Harkins in the dark about the coup d'état in Vietnam;

119

— destroying the November 1963 White House tapes under his custody;

— misleading and misrepresenting NSAM 273 by adding an Addendum on 11/21/1963 with an ominous warning of a threat to national security that urged everyone to unite and defend the United States government both here and in the field;

Mc George Bundy Was The Chief Assassin of Pres Kennedy

Water flows down a hill, heat travels from hot to cold and the second law of thermodynamics suggests Bundy was instrumental in the assassination of our 35th president John F Kennedy.

Consistent with the second law of thermodynamics all processes have a direction in life and the total sum of Bundy treacheries did kill JFK.

1. The reversal of JFK orders of air support for rebels at Bay of Pigs.
2. The cable to Amb. Lodge for a greenlight for a coup d'état in Vietnam. (August 24, 1963)
3. The personal note from his assistant Hillman to Amb. Lodge to authorize the coup d'état.
4. To keep general Harkins in the dark about the coup d'état in Vietnam.
5. To destroy November 1963 White House tapes under his custody.
6. To mislead and misrepresent NSAM 273 by adding an addendum on 11 /21 /1963 with an ominous warning of a threat to national security urging everyone to unite and defend the United States government both here and in the field.
7. To circulate a memo declaring the president's scheduled death the following day.

References
In retrospect ,Robert McNamara Random House 1996
JFK L Fletcher Prouty sky horse publishing 2006

120

— circulating a memo including the president's scheduled death the following day:

11/21/1963 draft
Top-Secret
National Security Action Memorandum Number 273

President has reviewed discussions of South Vietnam which occurred in Honolulu and has discussed the matter further with Amb. Lodge. He directs that the following guidance be issued to all concerned:

it is of the highest importance that the United States government avoid either the appearance or the reality of public recrimination from one part of it against another, and the president expects that all senior officers of the government will take energetic steps to ensure that they had their subordinates go out of their way to maintain and to defend the unity of the United States government both here and in the field.

— The president did not speak with Ambassador Lodge, because the president was in Texas and Ambassador Lodge in Honolulu; and,

— The president had no reason to order all senior government officials to unite and defend the US government the day before he died.

Are Lincoln And King Living Things?

Uncertainty is black
Waiting blue
Illusion is hope
Is believing Jefferson
Or Constitution
Or reason
Insane?

Are Lincoln Kennedy King
Living things or statues
Fabulous marbles
Do they whisper or talk ?
They talk to me
I hear their voices
Some nights
Some black nights

I live and inhale
Souls spirits and blood
Of my Lincoln King and Kennedy
I talk back loud
"You are no stones
You are living things
Robust and living
My friends
My soulmates
Lincoln Kennedy King"

Ch. 21:
Why did Kennedy die?

50 years is not enough time in history to judge a human about his influence upon world events. My educated guess is JFK introduced a new paradigm for our planet. He promoted democracy and dialogue prior to military intervention also defined when and under what circumstances the United will start war.

JFK clearly defined the American leadership by practicing democratic ideals both at home and abroad. He believed that every human being was of equal moral worth and in respect between nations.

The United States of America must engage in military action only when the security of the nation was at risk. JFK's executive actions and NSAM 263, in particular, was a clear demonstration of his vision of the future of US foreign policy.

He viewed Vietnam as an unnecessary war precisely because the US national security was not at risk and democracy and free market economics were better weapons to fight communism than war. The pursuit of the Vietnam War illustrated JFK's wisdom in seeking to avoid it.

JFK threaten the status quo

JFK had other paradigm shifting ideas and had come very close to making major changes involving the fundamental architecture of the US security: A single system under the Chairman of the Armed Forces with CIA and NSA incorporated into the overall military structure.

The change would offer a major shift by avoiding the pitfalls of conflicting strategies being pursued by covert operations. There would be full accountability for military decisions by placing them in the hands of the Chairman of the Joint Chiefs of the Armed Forces, who would report to the Commander-in-Chief.

November 22, 1963 delayed the implementation of these ideas, so vital for US and democracy. And one of the consequences of the assassination has been the fear factor of not bringing these ideas up for national debate.

Let us examine this fairly obvious observation in more detail. JFK promoted total governmental transparency and accountability.

Three US presidents—Eisenhower, Truman and Kennedy—were concerned about the split in military decisions to compromise intelligent and effective decision-making by the Commander-in-Chief. Eisenhower's "Farewell Address" and Truman's *Washington Post* article a month after JFK's death eloquently articulate the absolute necessity for the executive power of a democratically elected president. Neither Eisenhower nor Truman had the opportunity to implement their ideas. JFK did.

Hope for the future of democracy

Today there is reason to be hopeful about democracy.

We are in an era of world communication that will make it impossible for misrepresentations not to be discovered even if they were constructed by brilliant architects

The images suggest JFK was killed by intelligent people with unique access to complex technology and also enjoyed public trust and authority only enjoyed by the highest levels of our government. This observation is a concern as well as hope. For, our system is sensitively dependent upon the integrity of our fellow men.

This is a chance to benefit from JFK's death. For instance, we may realize that even the best of the best of us—such as Chief Justice Warren—can be misled, manipulated or fooled by others. This means the urgent need to ensure transparency and accountability to protect institutional integrity.

To err is human. Governmental integrity matters. We shall learn.

Who killed Oswald

Was it JFK
Now a national treasure
Or Bundy, LBJ and Vietnam
What if we ask
Witnesses
Oswald killing Ruby
Before JFK fired
The magic bullet

Postscript for Kaleigh

Dear Kaleigh

When you grow up to lead our nation remember JFK. We are JFK.

If you decide to avoid politics it will be nice to remember coura-
geous people such as Mark Lane, David Talbot, Jim Garrison, Matthew
Smith, Stuart Galanor, L. Fletcher Prouty, Jim Marrs, Oliver Stone, Jim
Fetzer, Peter Dale Scott, Noel Twyman, Mark North, James Douglas
and others who investigated the truth despite being labeled as "conspiracy theorists" and condemned for their search for truth and justice
for JFK .

Alen J. Salerian, M.D.

Thank you JFK

May I thank you JFK
For dying young
Thank you for living
Thank you for touching
Us imperfect people
We damaged goods
We Irish Italian Jew
We gay gypsies and Arabs
We black brown yellow
Thank you for
Climbing Appalachian rocks
Thank you for visiting
FMC Butner prison

Bibliography

- Crenshaw, Charles A., *JFK: Conspiracy of Silence*. M.D. Signet. 1992.

- Douglass, James W., *JFK And The Unspeakable*. Simon & Schuster. 2008.

- Fetzer, James H., *Murder in Dealey Plaza*. Open Court/Catfeet Press. 2000

- Fetzer, James H., *The Great Zapruder Film Hoax*. Open Court/Catfeet Press 2003.

- Dankbaar, Wim, *Files on JFK*. 2008.

- Galanor, Stewart, *Cover-up*. Kestrel. 1998.

- Garrison, Jim, *On The Trail Of The Assassins*. Sheridan Square Press. 1988.

- Jones, Howard, *Death Of A Generation*. Oxford University Press. 2003.

- La Fontaine, Ray and Mary, *Oswald Talked*. Pelican publishing. 1996.

- Lane, Mark, *Rush To Judgment*. Thunders Mouth Press. 1992.

- Lane, Mark, *Plausible Denial*. Thunder's mouth Press. 1991.

- Lane, Mark, *Last Word*. Sky horse Publishing. 2011.

- Livingston Harrison Edward. *High Treason*. Carroll and Graf Publishers. 1992.

- Marrs, Jim, *Crossfire*. Carroll and Graf Publishers

- McNamara, Robert, *In Retrospect*. Vintage Books. 1995.

• Meagher, Sylvia, *Master Index To The JFK assassination Investigations*. The Scarecrow press. 1980.

• Mitchell, Melanie. *Complexity*. Oxford University Press. 2009.

• Newman, John. *Oswald and the CIA*. Skyhorse Publishing. 2008.

• North, Mark, *Act Of Treason*. Carrol and Graf Publishers. 1991.

• Posner, Gerald, *Case Closed*. Anchor Books. 1993

• Prados, John, *The White House Tapes*. The New Press. 2003.

• Prouty, L. Fletcher, *JFK: The CIA, Vietnam and the Plot to Assassinate John F. Kennedy*. Skyhorse Publishing 2009.

• Salerian Alen. J., *"President Kennedy's Postmortem Exam Is Invalid"*. Medical Hypotheses. June 2008.

• Salerian Alen. J., *"President Kennedy's Death:Neurotoxin Assisted"*. Medical Hypotheses. 2011.

• Salerian Alen J., *"Review of Mass Homicides Of Intelligentsia"*. Forensic Examiner. 2007.

• Scott, Peter Dale, *Deep Politics and the Death of JFK*. University of California Press. 1993.

• Smith, Matthew, *JFK: The second plot*. Mainstream Publishing. 1992.

• Smith, Matthew, *JFK: Say Goodbye to America*. Mainstream publishing. 2001.

• Smith, Matthew, *Conspiracy: The Plot to Stop the Kennedys*. Citadel Press. 2005.

• Trask, Richard, *Pictures of the Pain*. B. Yeoman Press. 1994

• Twyman Noel, *Bloody Treason*. Laurel Publishing. 1967.

• Weberman, Alan J. and Michael Canfield, *Coup D'état*. Quick American Archives. 1992

The boy Said Fear The Jungle

Life a journey
A journey through
Lushness
Tropical jungle
Gorgeous gorges
Dizzying falls
Giraffes prancing

A boy stopped me
Half monkey half boy
Just imagine how shocked I was
Conversing in English
And mix of hand motions
Amused I was
When he asked
Where I was from
"Never stop
Never halt
Move forward
Don't pick cherries
Giant bees singing
Begging pleading
Seducing you

Underwater caves
Never visit
Red yellow turquoise fish
Fiesta on icy slopes
Fearless Lords of Norway"
The little boy said

"And all because
I from Washington
You caution me
Not to live
Not to smell flowers"
"Yes" he said bluntly
"Scariest stories
Of hugest men
Lincoln JFK and King
Who did not fear

About the Author

Alen J. Salerian, M.D., is the President of Doctors for Equal Rights for Mental and Physical Pain. As a psychopharmacologist, he currently divides his energy between research and advocacy for people with chronic and mental pain.

He has practiced in Washington, DC, for four decades; taught at George Washington University Medical Center; served as the FBI's Medical Director of its Mobile Psychiatric Emergency Response Team and as Medical Director of the Salerian Center for Neuroscience and Pain.

He has published numerous articles in peer-reviewed journals, including *Lancet, Psychiatric Research, CNS Spectrum, Medical Hypotheses and Journal of Psychology* and *Clinical Psychiatry*.

He has contributed to *The Washington Post, The Los Angeles Times* and *USA Today*. His scientific contributions have been cited by others 224 times.

Dr. Salerian also appeared on CBS' "60 Minutes" and the BBC's "Panorama". Prior to this, he had published two books, *Viagra For Your Brain* and *Honest Moments With Dr. Shrink* (cartoons).

Index

145

Made in the USA
Columbia, SC
11 February 2025